W0016954

Faces and Places in America

CONTENTS

NATIONAL GEOGRAPHIC

Hampton-Brown

School Publishing

Final Syllable: Consonant + **le**

Look at each picture. Read the words.

Example:

app**le**

turt**le**

tab**le**

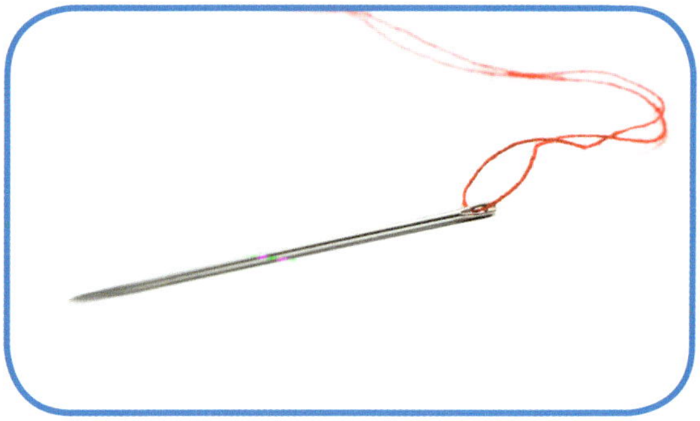

need**le**

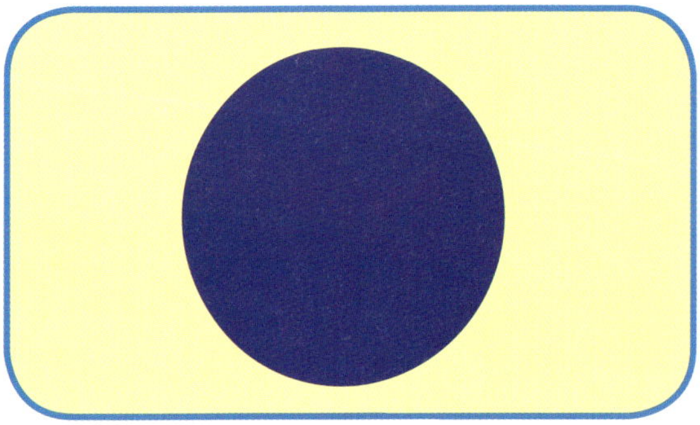

cir**cle**

bicy**cle**

High Frequency Words

example

got

music

sing

song

state

still

story

tell

today

Key Words

Look at the pictures. Read the sentences.

Washington State

1. Washington is a **state** in the Northwest.
2. Here is an **example** of a market in this state.
3. A shopper just **got** food there.
4. You can hear **music** in that state.
5. **Today** some singers **still** **sing** old songs.
6. A **song** may **tell** a **story**.

> Do you know where Washington is? Hint: It's on the West Coast.

Phonics Games

NGReach.com

3

Visiting Uncle Noble

by Tomas Fernandez
illustrated by David Lowe

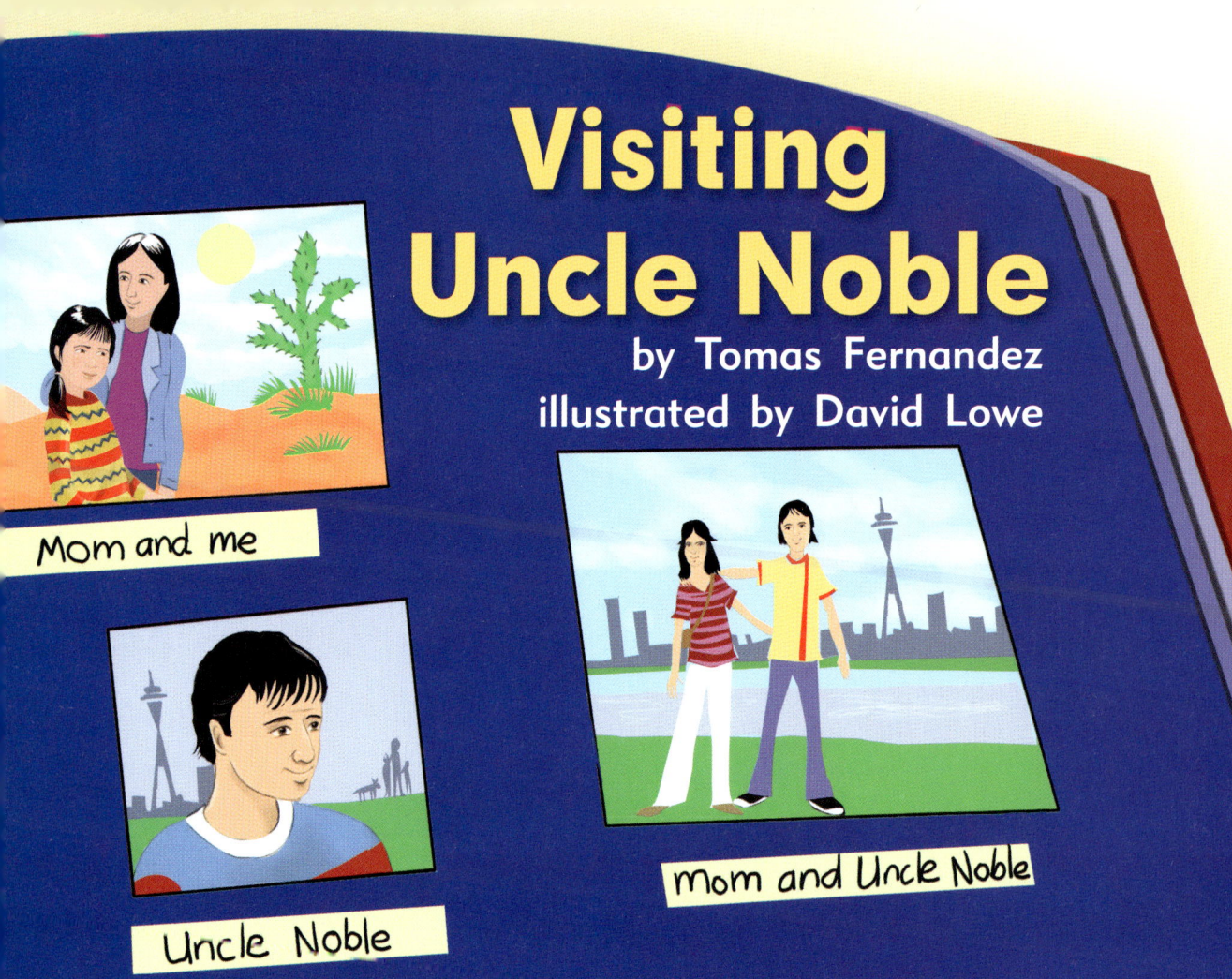

Mom and me

Uncle Noble

mom and Uncle Noble

Ester and her mother live in Texas, but Ester's mother grew up in Washington. When Ester was seven, they decided to visit Mom's brother, Noble. Uncle Noble still lived in Washington. Ester was excited. She would be able to learn more about where her family came from.

Uncle Noble lived in Seattle, Washington, the biggest city in the state. About 600,000 people live there. Ester made a map of the United States and drew a circle around Washington. She added a big purple dot for Seattle.

Can you find Seattle on the map?

Uncle Noble took Ester and her mom for a bicycle ride around Seattle. Mom wanted to see the Space Needle. She had loved to visit it when she was a girl. "I always thought it looked like something from outer space," she said.

What about you? Do you agree with Mom?

"Let's eat lunch at Pike Place Market, " Mom said to Uncle Noble. "People from all over the world settle in Seattle," she told Ester. "Some have shops in the market."

Uncle Noble, Mom, and Ester sat at a table. They ate noodles.

Later they got some fruit. Ester chose a pineapple. Uncle Noble got apples and some purple plums.

Uncle Noble asked, "Did you know that Washington produces more apples than the other states?"

"There used to be such great concerts in Seattle," Mom recalled.

"There still are!" exclaimed Uncle Noble.

That night, he took them to a concert. One band member shook a rattle as she sang a song.

"I like the way she sings!" Ester said.

One day Uncle Noble said, "Let's go to a rain forest. It's in a wet part of the state. More than 150 inches of rain may fall there each year."

The rain forest was a green jungle. Tangles of moss hung from maple trees. Jumbles of moss-coated branches lay on the ground. A drizzle of rain sprinkled everything. Puddles dotted the trail.

Ester watched beetles scuttle on the moss. Just then she whispered, "Did some leaves just crackle?"

"Elk are making that sound," said Uncle Noble. "See them?"

Later the sun sparkled in the sky. Ester saw a bald eagle flying high above.

"You know that we are Coast Salish, a tribe of the Northwest. Many of us are artists," Uncle Noble told Ester. "Did you know that your great-grandfather was a carver? He made tall totem poles out of wood."

"I knew he was a carver," said Ester. "But I've never seen any of his totem poles."

Ester saw an example of her grandfather's work. "It's amazing!" she cried.

"Carvers today still make totem poles the old way," Uncle Noble pointed out. "Each pole has a story behind it. It may tell about the tribe, the family, or the artist."

The week passed quickly. "Uncle Noble is lots of fun. I don't want to go home yet," grumbled Ester.

"I'll visit soon. Then you can show me around your state," said Uncle Noble.

"That's a deal!" said Ester. She knew lots of sights to show Uncle Noble.

Final Syllable: Consonant + <u>le</u>

Read these words.

rode	puddle	bicycle	saw	uncle
jungle	held	table	beetle	eagle

Find the words that end with a consonant + **-le**. Use letters to build them.

p	u	d	d	l	e

Talk Together

Choose words from the box above to tell your partner what each girl did.

> The girl <u>held</u> a <u>beetle</u> .

1.

2.

3.

Final Syllables with -tion, -ture

Look at each picture. Read the words.

Example:

ques**tion** mark

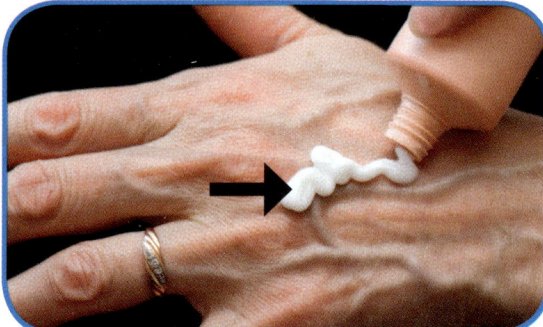

lo**tion**

frac**tions**

vul**ture**

pic**ture**

furni**ture**

High Frequency Words

High Frequency Words
example
got
music
sing
song
state
still
story
tell
today

Key Words

Look at the pictures. Read the sentences.

Examples of Culture

1. Some artists **today** keep cultures alive.
2. For **example**, they may **still** play old **music**.
3. They may **sing** an old **song**.
4. They may **tell** an old, old **story**.
5. This female artist **got** a prize for storytelling.
6. What cultures are in your **state**?

What can you tell others about your culture?

Phonics Games

NGReach.com

Keep Cultures Alive

by Tory Bonaventure

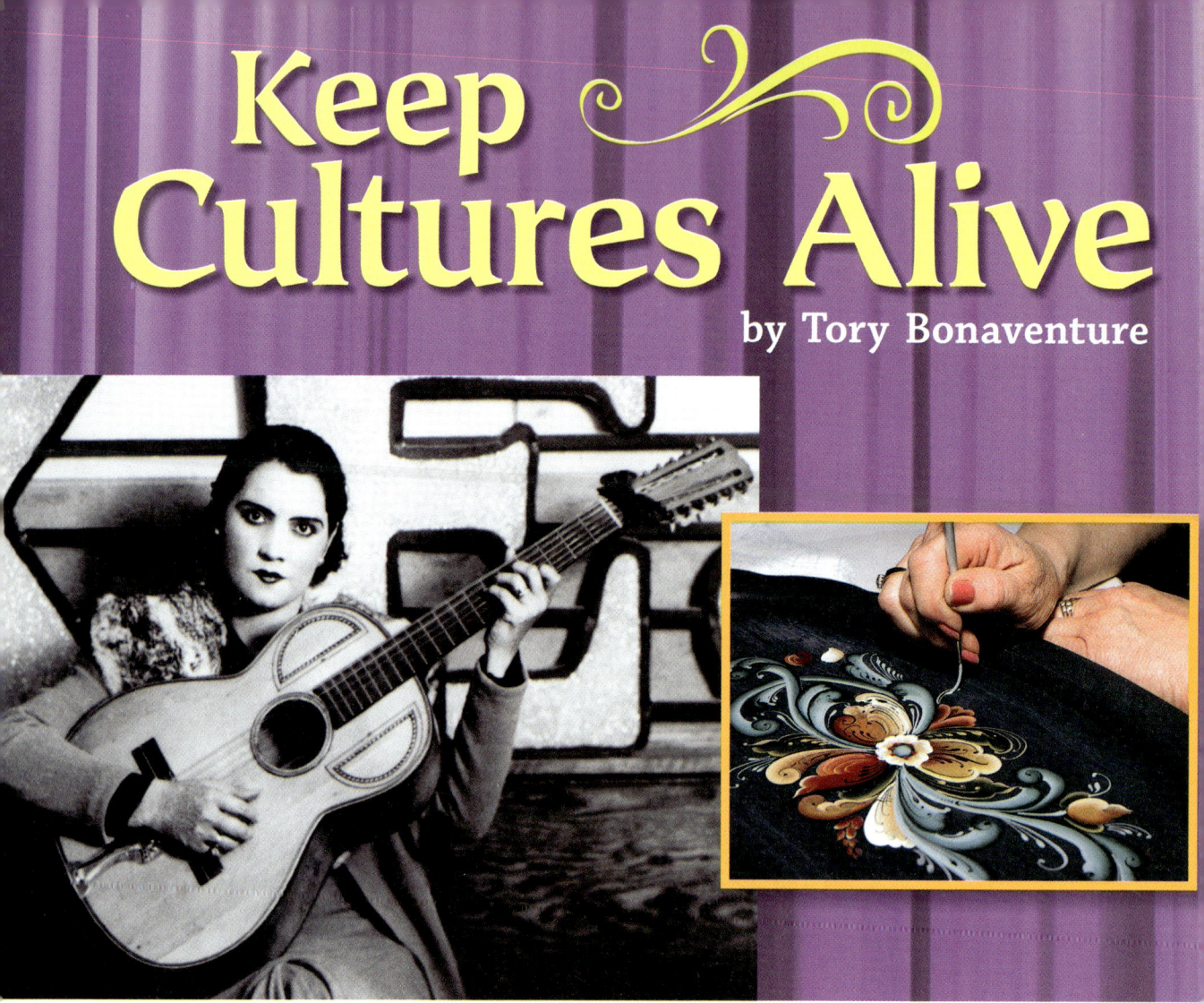

Each year since 1982, the United States gives fellowships to about 12 artists. A fellowship is a kind of prize. The artists are from many cultures. Different artists get the prizes each year. Some artists sing. Other artists have a craft. They may paint furniture.

The artists are quite good at their art or craft. But they also have made an important contribution to our nation. How? They keep their cultures alive. At the same time, they teach others about these cultures.

Sue Yeon Park

Korea

PACIFIC OCEAN

United States

Sue Yeon Park got a fellowship in 2008. She is a dancer and musician from Korea. Park shows her dedication to the art and music of Korea in many ways. She founded a group to teach young people the dances and music of Korea.

In addition, Park still dances and plays the music of Korea. She shares the arts of her culture with other people. She helps people learn about Korea's culture.

Domingo Saldivar

accordion

Texas

Domingo "Mingo" Saldivar got a fellowship in 2002. He is a well-known accordion player. Born in Texas, he plays a kind of Tex-Mex music. Tex-Mex music comes from his home state and Mexico. It started in the mid-1800s with the introduction of something new to those places— the accordion.

Saldivar likes to answer questions about his music. He explains that the songs he plays are stories about real life. For example, a song may tell a story about working in the fields.

Evalene Henry

Arizona

Evalena Henry is a basketweaver. She got a fellowship in 2001. Basket weaving is an old, old Apache art. Henry learned to weave baskets from her mother. Native American tribes used baskets for many things—even carrying water! The baskets were so tightly woven that moisture did not leak through.

Henry gives basket-weaving instruction to people. Her ambition is to keep the art of basket-weaving alive.

Look at the basket on page 24. What features do you see? Do you see the creatures? Does the basket have a bumpy texture or a smooth texture? What are your conclusions?

Philip Simmons

South Carolina

Philip Simmons got a fellowship in 1982. He trained as a blacksmith. He crafted fences, gates, and other objects from iron. Today you can see many of them in cities.

iron gate

Look at the picture. Simmons made this gate for a well-known institution. The gate has details that you might see in sculptures. Can you find the hearts?

Keeping cultures alive is a celebration of what makes our nation great. You have read about some prize-winning artists. You have seen how they use their art or craft to keep their cultures alive. What arts from your culture do you keep alive?

Final Syllables with -tion, -ture

Read these words.

nation	child	question	sculpture	contribution
furniture	artist	invention	culture	creature

Find the words with the final syllables **-tion** or **-ture**. Use letters to build them.

n a t i o n

Talk Together

Choose words from the box and either *a*, *an*, or no article to talk about what each person is making.

This child is making a creature.

1.

2.

3.

Wind

Help Uncle Find His Bicycle

Help Uncle Able find his bicycle. Follow the instructions. The steps tell you the route to take.

1. Pass a furniture store with a television in the window. It has a sale today.
2. Go up at the sculpture of an eagle and a turtle. It's in great condition!
3. Turn after you pass the musician playing fiddle music and singing a song.
4. Pass the picture of the bus station.
5. Pass a man who just got a mixture of pickles at a nearby shop.
6. Stay on the road. It leads to the bicycle.

Acknowledgments

Grateful acknowledgment is given to the authors, artists, photographers, museums, publishers, and agents for permission to reprint copyrighted material. Every effort has been made to secure the appropriate permission. If any omissions have been made or if corrections are required, please contact the Publisher.

Photographic Credits

CVR (bc) Jeff Greenberg/The Image Works, Inc. (br) Natalia Bratslavsky/Shutterstock. (cl) Paul Edmondson/Corbis. (tl) Alexander Gitlits/Shutterstock. (tr) Plush Studios/Blend Images/ Corbis. **2** (br) Lawrence Manning/Corbis. (cl) Simon Krzic/Shutterstock. (cr) Vladimir Koletic/ Shutterstock. (tl) Artville. (tr) Eric Isselée/Shutterstock. **3** (b) Liz Garza Williams/Hampton-Brown/National Geographic School Publishing. (tl) Richard T. Nowitz/Corbis. (tr) Chris Cheadle/ All Canada Photos/age fotostock. **15** (bc) Corbis RF/age fotostock. (bl) Image Source/Corbis. (br) Josh McCulloch Photography/Photographer's Direct. (cr) Liz Garza Williams/Hampton-Brown/National Geographic School Publishing. **16** (bl) C Squared Studios/Photodisc/Getty Images. (br) pics721/Shutterstock. (cr) Chris Johns/National Geographic Image Collection. (tr) Bork/Shutterstock. **17** (b) Liz Garza Williams/Hampton-Brown/National Geographic School Publishing. (tl) Nathan Benn/Alamy Images. (tr) Courtesy of the North Dakota Council on the Arts, photo by Troyd Geist. **18** (bg) OKRAD/iStockphoto. (cl) Michael Ochs Archives/Getty Images. (cr) North Dakota Tourism/Bruce Wendt. **19** James Wasserman Photography. **20** (bg) OKRAD/iStockphoto. (tl inset) Tom Pich Photography. (tl) Bakaleev Aleksey/iStockphoto. **21** (t) Tom Pich Photography. **22** (bg) OKRAD/iStockphoto. (tl inset) Richard Vasquez. (tl) Bakaleev Aleksey/iStockphoto. (tr) futureimage/iStockphoto. **23** Matt MacQueen. **24** (bg) OKRAD/ iStockphoto. (tl inset, tr) Tom Pich Photography. (tl) Bakaleev Aleksey/iStockphoto. **25** Nick Wass/AP Images. **26** (bg) OKRAD/iStockphoto. (tl inset) Tom Pich Photography. (tl) Bakaleev Aleksey/iStockphoto. (tr) Steve Lepre/Philip Simmons Foundation, Inc. **27** Steve Lepre/Philip Simmons Foundation, Inc. **28** (bg) OKRAD/iStockphoto. (cl) Bruno Morandi/age fotostock/ Photolibrary. (cr) Jed Share/Taxi/Getty Images. (tl) Birute Vijeikiene/Shutterstock. (tr) Steve Vidler/eStock Photo. **29** (bc) Tetra Images/age fotostock. (bl) Howard Grey/Getty Images. (br) Randy Faris/Corbis. (cr) Liz Garza Williams/Hampton-Brown/National Geographic School Publishing.

Illustrator Credits

4-14 David Lowe; **30-31** Peter Grosshauser

The National Geographic Society

John M. Fahey, Jr., President & Chief Executive Officer
Gilbert M. Grosvenor, Chairman of the Board

National Geographic School Publishing
Hampton-Brown
www.NGSP.com

Printed in the USA.
RR Donnelley,Menasha,WI

ISBN:978-0-7362-8085-3

11 12 13 14 15 16 17 18 19
10 9 8 7 6 5 4 3